The Word in this World

The Word in this World

Two Sermons
by
Karl Barth

Edited by Kurt I. Johanson
Translated by Christopher Asprey

REGENT COLLEGE PUBLISHING
Vancouver, British Columbia

Published 2007 by Regent College Publishing
5800 University Boulevard, Vancouver, BC V6T 2E4 Canada
Web: www.regentpublishing.com
E-mail: info@regentpublishing.com

Book design by Robert Hand
<roberthandcommunications.com>

Regent College Publishing is an imprint of the Regent Bookstore
<www.regentbookstore.com>. Views expressed in works published by
Regent College Publishing are those of the author and do not necessarily
represent the official position of Regent College <www.regent-college.edu>.

ISBN-10: 1-57383-411-4
ISBN-13: 978-1-57383-411-7

Cataloguing information for this title is available from
Library and Archives Canada Cataloguing in Publication

Contents

Gratis

120525

Foreword

From early on one of the elemental convictions of the theologian Karl Barth was that the same God who had spoken clearly the testimonies of the Holy Scriptures speaks also to us today. Therefore he formulated as a basic principle to be heeded precisely: "Preaching aims at the people of a specific time to tell them that their lives have their basis and hope in Jesus Christ" (*Homiletics*, trans. Geoffrey W. Bromiley and Donald E. Daniels [Louisville: WJK Press, 1991], p. 89). And even more: it is the task of preaching to state clearly that God himself makes himself heard in the contemporary situation. This task, according to Barth, is not well undertaken when a person thinks that God spoke once earlier and now this is to be carried forward and applied through the preacher in the present. The danger would then be too great that the preacher would play the role him/herself as the intermediary between God and humans or that the congregation would be kept busy with merely human opinions. According to Barth, the question is much more whether with the whole congregation the preachers also *hear* and pay attention to what *God* says—not only *said*, but *says*. Barth learned from the Reformers that the sermon in the service of worship is to correspond to the *prophetic* office of Jesus Christ.

However, according to him, this concept can also be said the other way round: The congregation hears God's word only when it listens to the word of God, who has already spoken according to the testimony of the Holy Scriptures. God has spoken not merely once, but rather once for all. If a person fails to pay attention to this, that person could lapse into a coarse or fine arbitrariness. Therefore the sermon should be guided by the Holy Scriptures. It documents this by beginning with the reading of a passage. The Bible text that is read does not have the function of a motto with which a person decorates self-invented thoughts. The first criterion of a true sermon is that it follows the Bible text that is its foundation; and everything it has to say and how it presents it is good so far as it follows its sermon text. Barth puts it thus: "The text itself must always be the master…" as contrasted to "what the great public, the smaller congregation, or our own heart might like to hear" (*op. cit.* 93, 95f.).

In the following pages are two sermons of Karl Barth to read. They come from different times of his life. He preached the first as a twenty-six year old pastor in the Swiss town of Safenwil, moved by the news recently announced in the newspapers of the sinking of the huge luxury liner, the Titanic. The second he delivered as a forty-eight year old professor of theology in Bremen; two days earlier the German Confessing Church, organized during Hitler's rule, had taken the dangerous step of speaking out against the Nazi government, and two days later Barth, because of his criticism of the church's accommodation to the political power, was relieved of his position in the university.

Both sermons proclaim the word of God as a relevant word. Each communicates clearly in its unique situation. Barth often offered as the rule of theological communication: it is appropriate time and again to say "the same thing differently." He says it in the first sermon obviously differently than in the later sermon.

The question is, nevertheless, whether he actually says the same thing in the first sermon or something different. The difference between the two sermons is clear: in the first, the sinking of the ship is the real topic of the "proclamation." Over against that, in the second text the threatening event is similarly a "ship sinking," but it is only hinted at. In the first text the newspaper report leads the thought and is then also illuminated by biblical words. In contrast, in the second sermon the Bible text is clearly "the master" of the thought and so it has the freedom to illuminate the contemporary events and to orient them in the world. The two sermons of Barth are of interest to readers today because they show how Barth in the time between the two texts had newly learned that a preacher must earnestly be a "servant of the word of God."

Eberhard Busch
Goettingen, Germany
Translated by Bruce E. Shields

Preaching with Karl Barth [1]

The main value of Karl Barth for us contemporary preachers is that he is a theologian.

I mean that statement to be deceptively simple. Of course, Karl Barth is one of the church's greatest theologians. We all know that. What we preachers must now relearn is that Karl Barth was *a theologian*—he never took his eyes off the central subject of truly Christian preaching, the one God who meets us as Father, Son, and Holy Spirit. Through a lifetime of preaching, theological reflection and writing, Barth consistently allowed the triune God who is revealed in scripture to govern his thought. The major reason why Karl Barth continues to be so interesting for us preachers who dare to read Barth is that Barth keeps reminding us of what a joy it is to talk about this God rather than to speak only of ourselves and our idols. I've spent a long time reading Barth and I love him, but Karl Barth is not nearly as interesting as what God said and showed Karl Barth about God. Like John the Baptist in Matthis Grünewald's "Crucifixion" of Colmar (his favorite painting), Barth kept

---

[1] This essay is a sort of distillation of my *Conversations with Barth on Preaching* (Nashville: Abingdon Press, 2006) in the light of two of Barth's famous sermons.

pointing, in everything he wrote, to the relentlessly self-revealing God who spoke to us as Jesus Christ.

Perhaps you would have to be a preacher to know why Barth's being a resolute theologian is his greatest gift to contemporary preaching. It's not only that much contemporary theology languishes in the realm of theologies-of-this-and-that, but also that much of contemporary theology appears to have forgotten both the proper subject and the vital agent of Christian preaching.

Forgive me for having this so prominently on my mind, but I have just finished listening to the sermons of sixty of the preachers who are under my care. Many of the sermons were lively and engaging and most congregations would hear them gladly on a Sunday morning. Yet in a depressing majority of them there was little indication that the content of the sermon or the engine driving the proclamation was the gospel of Jesus Christ. Other than that, most were fine sermons.

One sermon began well enough, the Second Sunday of Christmas, Luke 2, young Jesus putting the temple elders through their paces, abandoned by Mom and Dad. After reading the text, and noting Jesus' amazing ability to stupefy professional scholars, the preacher then sailed off into a veritable shopping list of things we needed to do. We were told that we needed to resolve, in the coming year, to be more proficient in study of God's word. We should all strive to "increase in wisdom and in stature." We ought to spend more time with our families.

Note how quickly, how effortlessly, and predictably the preacher disposed of a story about Jesus and transformed it into a moralistic diatribe about us. Moving from a text that simply declares what Jesus did and, by implication, who Jesus is, the preacher moved to a moralistic list of all the things that we need to do if we (in the absence of a living, active God) are to take charge of our lives and the world.

This is what Barth condemned as "religion," defined in *Romans* as "a vigorous and extensive attempt to humanize the divine,… to make it a practical 'something', for the benefit of those who cannot live with the Living God, and yet cannot live without God…."[2]

Of course, most congregations that I know love such sermons. The subtext is always, *You are gods unto yourselves. Through this insight, this set of principles, this well applied idea you can save yourselves by yourselves.* Whether preached by an alleged theological conservative or a liberal, there is a sense in which we're all Schleiermachians now. God is humanity spoken in a resonate, upbeat voice backed up with PowerPoint presentation. Reaching out to speak to the world, we fell in face down. Too troubled by our expectations of what our audience could and could not hear, we reduced the gospel to a set of sappy platitudes anybody could accept and no sensitive, thinking person could resist. Our testimony got reduced to whatever the market could bear. In the process of such "preaching," distinctive Christian speech was jettisoned and the discourse of pragmatic, utilitarian, therapeutic deism became the dominant homiletic mode. Finney's pragmatism and utilitarianism triumph. We thus violated Barth's "first axiom of theology"—the First Commandment, "thou shalt have no other gods before me."

---

[2] Karl Barth, *The Epistle to the Romans*, trans. Edwyn C. Hoskyns, 6th ed. (London: Oxford University Press, 1933), pg. 332.

I don't believe that I would have known any of this had not Barth told me that the Bible was more interesting than I could ever hope to be:

> Preachers must not be boring. To a large extent the pastor and boredom are synonymous concepts. Listeners often think that they have heard already what is being said in the pulpit. They have long since known it themselves. The fault certainly does not lie with them alone. Against boredom the only defense is again being biblical. If a sermon is biblical, it will not be boring. Holy scripture is in fact so interesting and has so much that is new and exciting to tell us that listeners cannot even think about dropping off to sleep.[3]

Scripture keeps preaching theological because it is of the nature of scripture to speak primarily about God and only secondarily or derivatively about us. Barth managed always to be obsessed by the biblical text—even as an experienced hermenute, he is continually stunned and delighted by the sheer otherness of the biblical text. Over the years I have enjoyed studying some prescribed lectionary text by first examining the text through various contemporary commentaries and then, using a scriptural index, turning to Barth's exposition of that text in his *Dogmatics*.[4] For us preachers, searching for something

---

[3] Barth, *Homiletics*, trans. Geoffrey W. Bromiley and Donald E. Daniels (Louisville: WJK Press, 1991), pg. 80.

[4] Barth's editors and translators, G. W. Bromiley and T. F. Torrance, compiled a wonderful resource for preachers, *Church Dogmatics: Index Volume with Aids for the Preacher* (Edinburgh: T. & T. Clark, 1977), that not only gives us a complete index of scripture and subjects in the *Dogmatics* but

to say, Barth declares, "The message which Scripture has to give us, even in its apparently most debatable and least assimilatable parts, is in all circumstances truer and more important than the best and the most necessary things that we ourselves have said or can say."

In seminary, someone had told me to "share myself," to build on my "life experiences" and thereby "connect with the congregation." Trouble was, I walked into my first parish at twenty-five. A few weeks peering into their lives convinced me that there was too little of myself to share. My life experiences were no match for the depth of their need and desire. Fortunately, this was about the time that I finally got around to reading Barth's *Epistle to the Romans*. Even my jaded, dulled post-graduate mind could see that I had come to a collision with much that I had been taught in seminary and grad school. I, who had invested a good deal in learning the ancient language and the historical context of scripture was told by Barth, in the preface, "I entirely fail to see why parallels drawn from the ancient world...should be of more value for an understanding of the Epistle than the situation in which we ourselves actually are."[5] So much for the historical-critical method! Barth then went on to ridicule much

---

also a rich selection of exegetical and expository texts from the *Dogmatics* that are keyed to the assigned scripture texts in the German Lutheran lectionary. This is a necessary volume for any preacher who would preach with Barth. *Karl Barth: Preaching Through the Christian Year*, ed. John McTavish and Harold Wells (Grand Rapids: Wm. B. Eerdmans Pub. Co., 1978) contains a judicious selection of passages from the *Church Dogmatics* that are keyed to the seasons of the liturgical year for use by preachers in the preparation of sermons.

[5] Preface to the Second Edition, pg. 11.

that I had been led to believe was a necessary prelude to saying anything in the pulpit.

More positively, Barth simply began his exposition of *Romans* without any prolegomena, with no effort to contextualize either Paul or himself, without speculation about theological antecedents, without assuming any theological prior development for what Paul had to say, and with a studied attempt not to anticipate what he would hear. He simply began where the epistle began and worked from there, verse-by-verse, continually surprised and delighted by what Paul said. I had never been in the presence of anyone who took the Word of God that seriously, or in that sort of way.

I realized, reading *Romans* in rural Georgia, that most of my hermeneutical training began with a sense of scarcity, a sense of want: With the biblical text, we lack the historical background, we don't have the linguistic skill to hear the text speak. Furthermore, biblical writers don't give us enough to go on in order to understand what they are talking about. We always must begin with them mid-argument, without sufficient understanding of the questions they were answering. No wonder it seemed as if we contemporary preachers had nothing to preach; we had nothing to hear.

Barth began with an assumption of abundance. In *Romans* Barth ridiculed Luther's love of the *deus absconditus*.[6] Barth begins with the assumption that God speaks, God reveals, that theology is, of necessity, always a work in process here, now. In Jesus Christ there is a decisive and irrefutable, constant and ever

---

[6] *Romans*, pg. 42.

present event of unveiling. Barth handles scripture as if scripture is handling him, as if the text is throbbing with revelation, as if there is a surfeit of divine knowledge, as if our dilemma is not that we can't hear God but rather that, in scripture, God is billowing over us with wave after wave of dramatic, stunning self-disclosure. God says too much to us, more than we can possibly assimilate. Even after we've said a great deal about the Trinity, there is a surplus of meaning left over. After the Resurrection, we've always had more future with God than past. No wonder Barth wrote such long books, and so many of them; the voice of God is so gloriously fecund that talk about God is never done. When we're working with such a self-revealing God, there is always something else for a preacher to say next Sunday.

At twenty-five, I decided that I had better get busy and start listening, start preaching, and pray that God would give me enough time to preach even half the sermons that God would give me.

We preachers are still being encouraged to begin our homiletics from a presupposition of lack and want. We are told that, if we would preach, we need a better theory of how to use the devices of rhetoric in order to move and to transform our congregations. We need a better understanding of the spiritual dilemmas of people who live in Des Moines. We need to utilize technology in our presentation of the gospel, blending the gospel with an astute reading of contemporary life, attempting to perform "culturally relevant" preaching. We must devise better metaphors and images than the ones that Jesus gave. Preaching is very hard work, coming up with something to say, because

God refuses to speak and, if God ever did, it is very difficult for us sophisticated modern people to hear.

Barth wouldn't understand any of this. Barth believes that we've got more gospel than we can possibly bring to speech. God has said so much, and spoken in such a fertile, thick, multivalent manner, that we've got more than enough to say right now, right here. Barth claimed that theology was a form of prayer—open-handed reception of the lavish gifts that God gives. And preparation for preaching is prayer too.

God is always the problem with preaching. We cannot let preaching be dominated by a humanly derived "how?" when our greatest challenge, and the source of our true power to preach, is the divinely given "Who?" Faithful preaching is that which has been theologically authorized. What difference does it make that we preach in the name of a Triune God whose nature is to speak? "And God said…" is the basis of everything. Can it be that our principles for better living delivered in PowerPoint, our "culturally relevant" communication techniques, are just our latest attempts to keep a living, speaking, strange God at a distance? Barth's homiletic implies a lively, impassioned plea for us preachers to return to the proper subject of our testimony— the Trinitarian God who refuses to be silent or to abandon us to our own rhetorical devices.

Preaching is the major reason why Barth began his massive *Church Dogmatics* with the longest exposition of the Trinity in modern times. If we do not have a God who speaks, then we really have nothing to say, much less anything to think about God. Christ is called the "Word." It is Christ who preaches before we preach. Everything is set in motion with the primal, Genesis claim, "And God said...." Barth's robust view of an active, unfailingly surprising, living God puts Barth at some distance from lots of the sermons that I hear and many that I preach. God too often enters the sermon as some sort of vague mystery about whom little is to be said. So we must quickly abandon the text and sail by the seat of our pants, offering exclusively human advice derived from limited human experience. There is a modern sort of modesty that refuses to claim too much for God. Presuming to be intellectual integrity, this reticence to do theology is in most cases the simple fear that to speak decisively about who God is and who God isn't would endanger our godlike aspirations to run the world as we damn well please. Thin descriptions of God are killing our sermons.

I love the two sermons that are included in this volume and find both of them, in vastly different ways, to be encouraging for a contemporary preacher. Having heard of Barth's "Titanic" sermon—through Barth's later lament over having preached it in his misspent youth—I loved reading it here. It is a remarkable sermon. Those of us who know mainly the later, *Church Dogmatics,* post-*Romans* Barth, have the greatest of difficulty believing that it came from Barth. The sermon is just about everything that Barth came to despise and to ridicule in his *Homiletics*—relevant, long introduction, mired in the merely contemporary, ranting against rapacious capitalism, finally remembering to say something about God at the end. You would have to be a preacher to know how deeply comforting it is to know that Barth once preached a sermon like this—a sermon as bad as anything I preached last month.

And yet the "Titanic" sermon is touchingly pastoral, in many of the ways that Barth would condemn being "pastoral." Here is a young pastor who is obviously overwhelmed by a contemporary tragedy. His people are asking, "Why?" and he takes their question seriously. Although his response to their "Why?" is not all that interesting, certainly not very theological, every preacher I know has had the experience of being overwhelmed by the immediate concerns of a congregation. To be a preacher is usually to be a pastor and pastors have a front row seat on the average pain and mundane despair that often afflict people. Sometimes, the most difficult thing for a pastor is to climb out of the quicksand of a congregation's pain long enough to say something theological, to not be totally engulfed by human pain.

After the tragedy on 9/11, I edited a collection of sermons that were preached by college chaplains and pastors on the Sunday after 9/11—*The Sunday After Tuesday: College Pulpits Respond to 9/11*.[7] Most of the sermons, including my own, attempted to bring the Christian faith to bear on the tragic, horrifying situation that had occurred in New York. What struck me was a sermon that I received from one of the chaplains at Notre Dame University. In his sermon for the day the preacher began by saying something to the effect that it had been a big week, but that meant that the church had much work to do on Sunday. So let's get right to the assigned gospel for the day. He read the gospel and preached a sermon that simply walked through the biblical text. It was a most "Barthian" sermon by a Roman

---

[7] (Nashville: Abingdon Press, 2002).

Catholic, a sermon that took the biblical text more seriously than any assumptions about the pastoral context. Refusing to be jerked about by the headlines for the week, the preacher honored the gospel for the week and worked from there. In the sermon, scripture was taking time, scripture was naming our plight, setting our agenda. I could see Barth smiling.

Barth's sermon from the Frauenkirche on Matthew 14 is a classic, remarkable not only for what it says, but even more remarkable when set next to the "Titanic" sermon. I met Barth as a preacher in his collection of sermons in English, *Deliverance to the Captives!*[8] Those sermons were preached in the jail at Basel and show the preaching of the later Barth. The Matthew 14 sermon is typical of Barth's "prison sermons," though a bit more detached from the congregation than those sermons, more studiously committed to a verse-by-verse commentary on a biblical text, longer, and full of serious intent. Here is Barth exemplifying the principles of his lectures on preaching that were delivered at about the same time in Bonn, the lectures that became his great homiletical *tour de force, Homiletics.*

Preached under the gathering storm clouds of Nazism, there is no mention of Nazis or Hitler. Here is Barth following his own advice to the German church when he was expelled from his professorate at Bonn—"exegesis, exegesis, exegesis." He is preaching, as he urged, "as if nothing had happened." The "nothing" is Hitler and Barth refuses to let him or his minions enter the sermon. The sermon begins without introduction or any attempt to lure the congregation into the text. It feels

---

[8] Karl Barth, *Deliverance to the Captives!*, trans. Marguerite Wieser, (New York: Harper, 1961).

as if the text has just been dropped, like a meteor, in the middle of a congregation. The preacher begins, as it were, in mid-conversation, holding up the jewel of the text before the congregation, admiring every strange facet of its brilliance. Here is a preacher who is more fascinated by the ancient text than by the contemporary congregational context.

No, that is not quite fair to Barth. Because of his theology, it is as if the seriousness of the congregational context drives him to the text. Matters have become so dangerous for the German church that Barth dare not take his eyes off a God who saves, who judges, who teaches, who kills and makes alive. Working in a line-by-line exposition of the dramatic story, Barth marvels at the movements of the God who commands his disciples get into a boat and steer into the storm. The way to counteract paganism in the form of National Socialism is by close, obedient attentiveness to another God. The very form and structure of the sermon is itself a kind of theological claim. Barth submits to the text, allows the text to take charge, to have authority over anything that will be said or thought in Bremen on that day. Barth claims, in this sermon, that we need not fear. God will speak to us, in the night, in the storm. And the word God speaks is a life-giving, victorious word.

It is fine for us preachers to try to speak to the culture, to try to make our sermons relevant to the needs of our people. But what does a preacher say when the sky is dark, very dark, and the temptations are so seductive, and the Enemy puts on a polite, benign nationalistic smile telling us that there are some sensible measures that need to be taken because our culture, our nation, our way of life are being threatened? In such a time, it is as if the preacher, in true service to the congregation, is driven to the text, the authoritative text that stands above our context, the text that speaks a word that we, in our fearful situation, could never speak to ourselves. This is the birth of truly faithful preaching. And this is the witness who is Karl Barth.

I am resisting the temptation to lament that in our present age, when torture is defended by a government that claims its greatest interest is in spreading democracy, when democracy is considered a higher attainment even than Christianity, when we are revealed to be a very fearful people who, in our fear, are willing to sacrifice our children, our future, all in the interest of "security," well, Barth's sermon at the Frauenkirche is a slap in the face. Here we are, all safe and secure on the shore, then Jesus commands us to get into the boat and to sail into the storm. We are a profoundly insecure people and the source of our insecurity is revealed to be not Islamic terrorists but rather the God who commands us in Jesus the Christ. I'm therefore hearing Barth's sermon as a call across the years, across the waves and the wind, to be the preacher that God has called me to be.

Preach on, Karl Barth.

William H. Willimon

Acknowledgements

"It is always better to read Karl Barth than to read about him. He has a wonderful way of dispelling any caricatures that may have arisen at second hand." *George Hunsinger*

"In the English-speaking world Barth has yet to be assimilated fully. It may well be that the period of his greatest influence lies in the future." *Bruce McCormack*

"In a very real sense all of Barth's theological work has been dedicated to the service of the pulpit." *William Hordern*

Ever mindful that these two distinctly different sermons by the Swiss Pastor-Professor Karl Barth included in this booklet, and released for the first time in English translation, were both born out of world-wide tragedy and crisis, it is my hope that those who were among "the drowned and the saved" on the Royal Mail Ship Titanic, and those who traded time for eternity in the fiery furnace of the Fuhrer, will always be remembered and never forgotten. This booklet, and the extra-ordinary effort(s) to produce it, is an attempt to honor their memory. It is also a clarion call to the pastors who herald the glorious gospel of our God from the pulpit, and to those who hear it in the pew, to powerfully proclaim and witness to the Word in this world.

Let me briefly describe the path to production of "The Booklet."

The origin or idea of The Booklet took place in both a Lecture Hall and a chapel at Bowie Divinity House at Erskine Theological Seminary in Due West, SC (Due West of what? I do not know). In October 2004, I was sitting in on a doctoral course in Expository Preaching taught by the homiletical historian from Princeton, Hughes Oliphant Old, when it was announced that Eberhard Busch was to deliver a lecture entitled "Seven Theses on Preaching." This lecture was a summary of Karl Barth's theology and theory of proclamation. The lecture offered a rare glimpse into a "strange new world" I had not previously visited.

On the flight home I thought about the mountain of manuscripts produced during the last few decades in the scriptoria of scholars—both appreciative and highly critical— on Barth's position(s) and thought(s) on a variety of issues in his vast literary corpus. But something has been missing. Where are the essays, the lectures, the manuscripts, dealing with Barth's theology of proclamation? After all, did not Barth state that his theology was written to inform proclamation and be of service to the church in this primary task of ministry (*The Word of God and The Word of Man* and also in *Church Dogmatics*)? Sure, we all have copies of *God's Search For Man*, *Come Holy Spirit*, *Deliverance of the Captives!*, and *Call For God*. Some of

us are fortunate enough to own the rare volume *Furchte Dich
Nicht!* But what has been produced, in translation, since 1967?
Nothing![1]

Where are the Safenwil sermons? Where are the bold
declarations from Basel, Berlin, Bonn, and Bremen—the cutting
critique(s) of National Socialism and the strengthening words
to the Confessing Congregations? Where is the great Titanic
sermon?

So, in the first week of November 2004, I contacted
Geoffrey Bromiley, Barth's famed translator, to inquire about
Barth's preaching, and I had the audacity to ask if he could
help me understand Barth—all in the space of a brief phone
conversation! The first thing he said to me was that I should
read the sermon on the Titanic. What puzzled and troubled me
was that he said this while slowly laughing! And, after receiving
a copy of KBA 1089 from the KB-Archiv in Basel, I found
out why! Bromiley was right; his hand-writing is impossible to
decipher!

In addition to this providential phone conversation with
Geoffrey Bromiley, I read a section on "Europe in Crisis," by
Hughes Oliphant Old, where he identifies Barth's Bremen
sermon of Jesus walking on the water as "one of the outstanding
sermons of the twentieth century," and thought this would be a
good complement to the sermon on the sinking of the Titanic.[2]

---

[1] This void is now filled by William H. Willimon's volume, *Conversations
With Barth On Preaching* (Nashville: Abingdon, 2006).

[2] Hughes Oliphant Old, *The Reading and Preaching of the Scriptures
in the Worship of the Christian Church*, vol. 6, *The Modern Age 1789–1989*
(Grand Rapids: Wm. B. Eerdmans Publ. Co., 2007), pg. 776.

There it is. The birth of The Booklet! The rest of this section is humbly giving credit where credit is due:

From the beginning stages, to the eve of production, Clifford Anderson, Curator of Special Collections, Princeton, has been a constant help and invaluable resource; Clifford, I am grateful.

I would also like to thank Sarah Malone, Princeton, for her suggestion(s) of the images of Pastor-Professor Barth which we have used in The Booklet.

Thanks to Christopher Asprey, Aberdeen/London, for providing two excellent translations of these sermons by Barth. And to Eberhard Busch who transcribed Barth's "old gothic letters" to modern German for our translator.

Special thanks are due both to Hans-Anton Drewes and Dieter Zellweger, of the Karl Barth-Archiv, and the Karl Barth Legacy Commission, for permission to publish KBA 1089—"the monster of a full-scale Titanic sermon" (Karl Barth, *Homiletics* [Louisville: WJK Press, 1991], pg. 118). Thanks also to Revd. Zellweger for adding a word of commendation to this already fine piece.

Thanks is due to Marianne Stauffacher, Reference, TVZ (Theologischer Verlag Zurich), for granting permission to print Karl Barth's sermon on Matthew 14:22–33 (1934), previously in *Predigten 1921–1935*, herausgegeben von Holger Finze-Michaelsen, Abt. 1, *Karl Barth-Gesamtausgabe* (Zurich: Theologischer Verlag, 1988), pp. 342–357, and also *Fürchte Dich Nicht!* (Munich: Chr. Kaiser Verlag, 1949), pg. 18–31.

Thanks also to Kenneth Beken (Beken-of-Cowes-UK) who allowed us to use Frank Beken's photo taken on 10 April 1912 as the R.M.S. Titanic left Southampton harbor. Photo © <www. beken.com.uk>.

Bill Reimer, Robert Hand, and Rob Clements of Regent College—Thanks, again and again, for allowing me to produce and publish another excellent volume; I am doubly blessed to work with you!

Many thanks to Eberhard Busch for providing a fine Foreword to these sermons by Karl Barth. Thanks also to William H. Willimon (that peculiar prophet) for the excellent essay/contemporary reflection on "Preaching With Karl Barth." Thanks to Geoffrey Bromiley, James D. Strauss, and Donald McKim for their words of commendation. Special thanks is directed to Bruce Shields who translated Revd Zellweger's words and the *Vorwort* by Eberhard Busch from the German, and for proof-reading the texts and sermons. Thanks also to Pastors Russell Blowers and Warren Frederick Mathis of Indianapolis for their words of encouragement and prayers in the final stages of this work.

An additional word of thanks is offered to Donald Bloesch of Dubuque Seminary who has been, over the past fifteen years, a source of encouragement and grace, through both conversation and correspondence.

A heart-felt thanks is given to George and Jimmie Jo Grogan and Dan and Nita Bardsley, members of Pleasant Grove Christian Church (Dallas) who, for the past 10 years, have loved, prayed for, and welcomed my family into their own. This is, indeed, hospitality in the truest Christian sense.

Thanks always to "my beautiful bride" (as we say in Texas) Barb, and my two precious children—Garrett and Kiersten—

God's extra-ordinary, sweet, and absolutely undeserved gift to an ordinary man. In this aspect of life, I certainly out-kicked my coverage! All I can say is, "Wow-wee!"

Last, a word to the reader. Please know that I am Pastor at a small congregation in Dallas, Texas where I write these words and witness from the wasteland of a world that includes crisis and tragedy—burglaries, drugs, gangs, murder, over-crowded and poorly staffed schools, poverty, racial tension/immigration battles, and violence—as a part of everyday existence. I want nothing more than the church, and her scholar-preachers, to be able to offer, in one unified voice, as a part of her calling, a confident word to the world. It is my simple hope and prayer that the Pastor and the Professor can work together toward the recovery of courageous and powerful biblical preaching. I hope this Booklet provides a beginning.

I close with these words, from another Pastor-Professor, James S. Stewart, who wrote: "Certainly in these pages there is a Word from the Lord for the revitalizing of the Church."[3]

Kurt I. Johanson
Dallas, Texas
15 April 2007

---

[3] James S. Stewart, *Preface to Karl Barth: Prayer and Preaching*, trans. B. E. Hooke (London: SCM Press, 1964), pg. 8.

On the Sinking of the Titanic

21 April 1912

Above: The "R.M.S. Titanic"
(Courtesy of Beken-of-Cowes)

On the Sinking of the Titanic

Safenwil, Sunday 21 April 1912

Psalm 103.15–17
As for man, his days are like grass; as a flower of the field, so he flourishes. For the wind passes over it, and it is gone, and its place remembers it no more. But the mercy of the Lord is from everlasting to everlasting on those who fear him, and his righteousness to children's children. (NKJV)

Dear parishioners,

At the start of last week we were all taken aback by the news of the sinking of the English steamship "Titanic," bound for America, on which more than 1500 lives were lost in the waters of the Atlantic Ocean. And since then we have not been able to pick up a newspaper without learning new details about this catastrophe, whose proportions and circumstances are quite unique. I don't know whether this event has preoccupied you as much as it has me. If up until now it has not, then today I would like to encourage you to reflect on it. For I believe that, just as we may not approach events such as this one out of curiosity and a thirst for sensation, nor may we disregard them in silence and indifference, however much daily newspaper reports might cause us to do so. Rather, they should speak to us. For through them God addresses us with a power and urgency that we only rarely perceive: concerning the greatness and nothingness of human beings who are so like God, and yet so unlike him, concerning the wrath and the mercy of the eternal God who reigns in us and over our destinies, sometimes close at hand and tangibly, but sometimes infinitely far away and mysteriously. God speaks in this way even through a tragedy like the one which has shocked the entire civilised world this week, and we cannot fail to hear, nor may we.

Let us recall once more what we have chillingly witnessed. On Wednesday 10 April a ship left the port of Southampton in England for the first time, a construction the like of which the world had never seen before. For decades Germany and England have been competing to manufacture the largest, most comfortable and quickest ocean liner. Each has overtaken the other again and again. Five years ago in Hamburg, I had the chance to see one of these massive ships for myself, which at that time seemed to be the most enormous thing that human inventiveness and energy could create. But since then it has been easily overtaken by others. Fourteen days ago the Titanic, along with another English ship built identically, was now leading the field. A miracle of the modern human mind, which utterly surpasses even the most fantastical images any of us could conjure up, it has been appropriately called an amphibious town. Just imagine a ship that is 280 metres long and 30 metres wide. The lowest deck alone rises 20 metres above the water like a tower.

Three more decks tower above it, and beneath the waterline it descends to unfathomable depths, where there are storerooms and engine rooms, which one can imagine looking like a tall and spacious factory hall. A crew of 800 mans this monster, of which 300 work on the engines alone. Besides that, however, there are board and lodgings for 5000 passengers. And these passengers—those who can pay, at any rate—lack none of those finer things of life which they afford themselves on dry land. And so, there are on board: a garden restaurant, complete with trees and exotic creepers, a children's playroom, a swimming pool, Turkish and electric baths, a gallery with boutiques in which you can buy luxuries such as jewels and lace, a roller-skating rink, a gymnasium, a dancehall, a fish-pool for anglers, a theatre and another garden. Evidently, the travellers also enjoyed private cabins furnished with every comfort, excellent cuisine and all kinds of entertainment, none of which the finest hotel could provide better. It is like a dream world, all this refined ease and splendour floating on top of the unfathomable depths of the ocean, propelled by engines of 46,000 horsepower. In scarcely six days it was to reach New York and the quicker the better, as the captain well knew; every minute of speed on the journey was precious. For it was a matter of breaking the record, i.e., of cutting down even more, if possible, on the time it had taken other ships to cross, so as to get there in the quickest time yet. If it succeeded, the reputation of the shipping company that owned the Titanic would soar, and more importantly, so would its shares. And the captain must have done everything he could to achieve this target. It's just that he was even too eager. For the crossing from Europe to America is not as safe as we tend to think. Great masses of glacier ice broken off from the coast of Greenland are continually drifting southwards, not in small blocks but in massive fields and mountains, the great bulk of which, however, always floats under the surface of the sea. Cautious sailors will always cross this icy expanse with great caution, indeed they prefer to make a detour to avoid it. But taking caution and making detours was not consistent with the Titanic breaking the speed record, and so things had to be done differently. The ship motored at full steam day and night, and it took the most direct route. And so we come to last Sunday evening. The end was no longer far off. A few passengers were sitting, enjoying all manner of diversions; others had retired to their beds. At that moment they were disturbed by a jolt that shook the entire ship. But they hardly noticed it, since the ship was too big for people to realise what had happened at first. We hear stories of some people who calmly went on playing cards. The captain has the musicians on board strike up a merry tune. In reality, the front portion of the vessel has collided at full force with an iceberg floating under water, and it has been completely smashed up in a number of places. The formidable steel panels have been snapped like matchsticks, and with them all the safety measures are breached, and water is already pouring inside at full force. The disaster can no longer be covered up, and it is a matter of putting emergency plans into action. 2200 people are on board, yet there are only twenty lifeboats. One is astonished to read how the crew took up positions under orders from their officers to evacuate the boat as they had been drilled, how, without hesitation, men allowed women and children to go ahead of them to fill the spaces that were available, how the ship's musicians kept playing to provide a sense of calm assurance, how a brave officer kept the wireless telegraph transmitter going until the last minute, so as to send out a distress signal to every corner of the dark ocean. Help came, but it came too late: the nearest boat took four hours to arrive and could do nothing but take on board the 700 or so occupants of the lifeboats, who had half-died of cold. The Titanic itself had long since disappeared into the deep. It must have been a terrible sight when at last the whole ship, in the full glare of its electric lights, rose vertically out of the water once more, only to sink straight under. The last thing that was heard were a few pistol shots which are said to have been the captain taking his own life. We cannot imagine the scenes of horror and the deadly struggle that was played out inside, in the cabins and corridors, in the remotest reaches of the engine rooms. And now the Titanic and all its treasures, the wonders of its technology and design, its seven million letters to America, and above all its 1500 human lives, lies buried 4000 metres below the sea, in murky depths which have never seen a ray of light. And no one alive will ever set eyes on it again.

Indeed, *as for man, his days are like grass; as a flower of the field, so he flourishes. For the wind passes over it, and it is gone, and its place remembers it no more.* This terrible catastrophe proclaims that with an awful clarity. It is infinitely difficult to find the right words to express what these facts silently preach to us. We humans so easily become senseless and superficial when we have to speak about things like this, or else we make rash and presumptuous judgments, as if we had been sitting in the divine council when this incident was being ordained. And so I would like to tell you clearly but cautiously what thoughts and impressions this event has left with me. I know that whatever I can say will not suffice. Do not stop short at my words, then, but consider for yourselves what God wished to say to us through this.

First: the devastating impression of *the smallness and helplessness of humankind*, of everything its intellectual powers have created, and of the impressive advances made in this 20th century. You must understand me rightly when I say this. I fear that in many church pulpits today it will be claimed that such advances made in the perfecting of technology are somehow ungodly and even demonic, that a disaster such as this one reminds us again that God will have none of it. The simple-minded will draw the conclusion that it is a sin to build ships this big and to journey across the sea in them. Quite the reverse, I am saying. It is entirely God's will that the world's technology and machinery attain to higher degrees of perfection. For technology is nothing other than mastery over nature, it is labour, and the divine spirit in humanity ought to expand in this labour and to prosper. If people did not invent things, or if they did not wish to make proper use of things that have been invented, that would be the work of the devil. And therefore it is also entirely God's will that people build large, swift and comfortable ships, and venture out upon the seas in them. It is not at all religious, but utterly irreligious, to make the sign of the cross before this idea. But I nevertheless get the impression that in this disaster God has intended to show us once more that he is the boss. This is what I mean by that: there is a way of using technology that cannot be called labour any more, but *playful arrogance*. It is arrogance to install theatres and fish-pools on

Above: Facsimile of Barth's original hand-written notes on the Titanic Sermon
(Courtesy of Special Collections, Princeton Theological Seminary Libraries
on behalf of *Karl Barth Stiftung* of Basel, Switzerland)

a vessel exposed to these sort of risks, as is obviously still the case today with an ocean steamship. It is arrogance, because mind and body and money are being expended upon luxury and frivolities instead of on safeguarding against such disasters. Dancing and putting on plays and fishing, when one has not yet made sufficient provision for being caught out by icebergs: that is called acting in total assurance, as if there were nothing left to discover. There is a lie to be seen in the contrast between all the fuss and bother on board this ship and the helpless way in which it then had to submit to a very elementary force of nature. The catastrophe brought this lie to light. God will not be mocked. He certainly intends us to work and to achieve something in the world. But he does not intend us to act as though we were done with working, and could now go fooling around. If *that* is what we will do, then *he* will be done with us. He does not always show us that. But sometimes he does, and he sends us an iceberg to remind us that we have no reason to play the fool, when we should be working and battling away. God has not set a limit to technology, to progress, to the human mind. Quite the reverse! They are called to immortality. But when we become godless about the headway we have made, i.e. when we become bumptious and conceited and childish, then we need to be called to order. With all our understanding and progress, if we begin to feel unsure of ourselves once more, if we feel something of the gravity of our situation again—

> Midway through the course of life,
> When death doth us surround,
> Whom may we call upon to help,
> Where is mercy to be found?

—then we are as God will have us, for then we do not spend our lives playing childish games, but on things that are obviously serious and worthwhile. This is where he wants to lead us when he reminds us of our smallness and helplessness through tragedies like this.

Secondly: this disaster *did not have to happen.* If we have to say of the Titanic and its 1500 victims today, they are gone and their place remembers them no more, the blame for this lies with humanity. It is true that God set that iceberg on its course, but no one was compelled to get in its way. It is well worth considering how much intellectual brilliance and diligent hard work had gone into building this ship and making it as safe as possible. And again, how the passengers placed their complete confidence in the trustworthiness of those who had built it. But also, how this confidence was conditional on the trustworthiness of the 800-man crew, from the captain right down to the last boiler-man. That was all good and proper, and everything held together like links in a chain. Only there was one faulty link. The captain did not just have the safety of his passengers to think about, but also, and principally, the commission he had been given by the shareholders who were employing him, to break that speed record if he possibly could, on the ship's very first voyage. And it is because of this fragile link in the chain of trustworthiness, because of this guilt, that the Titanic went under, along with 1500 human beings. And it is on this guilt which ran the Titanic into the iceberg that we must now reflect. We will certainly apportion only the smallest measure of it to the unfortunate captain, who was an old man and intended that the first voyage of this new ship would be famous for being his last. Even though he took his own life, he now stands before a higher judge who judges according to more lofty standards than we could. But those who are guilty are the ones who made this a fragile chain by charging the old man with these orders: i.e., the shipping company whose president was also travelling on the Titanic and is among those who have been rescued—unfortunately, we are almost tempted to say. It is these people who saw this expensive ship, and all the intellectual effort which went into building it as well as the 800 sailors and 1400 passengers on board, as a great money-making operation. It is they above all who placed the safety of 2200 lives beneath their desire to compete with other companies. It is they who, for the sake of their dividends, have 1500 dead people on their consciences, together with all the distress this has brought upon families on both sides of the ocean. But ultimately not even this shipping company bears all the guilt for this disaster, but first and foremost the system of acquisition by which thousands of companies like this one are getting rich today, not only through shipping but across the whole spectrum of human labour. Yesterday in the "Freier Aargauer" newspaper the sinking of the Titanic was referred to as a *crime of capitalism*. After everything that I have now read about it I can only agree. Indeed, this catastrophe is a crude but all-the-more clear example to us of the essential characteristics and the effects of capitalism, which consists in a few individuals competing with each other at the expense of everyone else in a mad and foolish race for profits. Exactly the same course of events has already been played out in many other areas of labour. Indeed, it is almost tempting to interpret every feature of this catastrophe symbolically: the ship of human workers races onwards, but it is not consideration for the many which is at the helm, but the self-interest of the few. What about the engines? What about the people? The engines and the people are only machines for making money. The sinking of the Titanic teaches us where this ordering of society and labour will lead, if we have not already learnt this anywhere else. This is the fragile link in the chain of trustworthiness. As long as self-interest is not now eradicated and replaced by the idea of one-for-all and all-for-one; as long as we do not now repent and strive for a truly communal labour, we run the risk of conjuring down upon ourselves calamities of a quite different sort than the sinking of the Titanic.

But in spite of the sin and guilt of humanity which we see reflected in this event, we may now draw attention to the other side of the matter, as it is raised specifically by this event as well: *But the mercy of the Lord is from everlasting to everlasting on those who fear him, and his righteousness to children's children.* It is God's mercy that gives us hope in spite of sin and guilt. It creates in us the faith and childlike confidence which overcome sin and guilt, and build up the kingdom of God. So this shipping disaster doesn't merely point up our helplessness and our faults, our broken arrogance and our secret egotism. Nor does this [mercy] just proclaim to us our transience and its cause. It declares to us with a clarity we rarely experience that God's purposes are advancing in the world. One senses something of how Christ is becoming an ever greater force in the world, when one reads of those who did not seek to save themselves but did their duty, who ultimately did all they could, not for themselves but for others, who silently and nobly retreated in the face of death to allow those who were weaker than them to continue on the path of life. In view of facts such as these, it takes great unbelief to keep referring to our age as evil and godless. No, the mercy of the Lord is from everlasting to everlasting; it shone through the death and destruction of this disaster, so that we are grateful to be able to see it so plainly. In the attitude and conduct of those ordinary sailors during the most severe hour of testing, we see once again a sign of the new heaven and the new earth for which we are waiting. People will labour just as they did, when one day they will not labour for their own interests but as citizens of God's kingdom. This sign must not pass us by in vain. These courageous and selfless people must not be allowed to have drowned at sea for nothing. Rather, the message of God's mercy from everlasting to everlasting, which they have proclaimed to us, should prick our hearts and consciences; it should rouse us, shake us and get us up on our feet. It should lead us out of our mortality and sin to righteousness. If it does that, then we will not forget this horrifying event. Amen.

The Bremen Sermon

24 November 1934

Above: Barth in the pulpit
(Courtesy of Special Collections, Princeton Theological Seminary Libraries
on behalf of *Karl Barth Stiftung* of Basel, Switzerland)

The Bremen Sermon

Church of U.L. Frauen, Bremen, 24 November 1934

Matthew 14.22–33

Immediately Jesus made his disciples get into the boat and go before him to the other side, while he sent the multitudes away. And when he had sent the multitudes away, he went up on the mountain alone to pray. Now when evening came, he was alone there. But the boat was now in the middle of the sea, tossed by the waves, for the wind was contrary. Now in the fourth watch of the night Jesus came to them, walking on the sea. And when the disciples saw him walking on the sea, they were troubled, saying, "It is a ghost!" And they cried out for fear. But immediately Jesus spoke to them, saying, "Be of good cheer! It is I; do not be afraid." And Peter answered him and said, "Lord, if it is you, command me to come to you on the water." So he said, "Come." And when Peter had come down out of the boat, he walked on the water to go to Jesus. But when he saw that the wind was boisterous, he was afraid; and beginning to sink he cried out, saying, "Lord, help me!" And immediately Jesus stretched out his hand and caught him, and said to him, "O you of little faith, why did you doubt?" And when they got into the boat, the wind ceased.

Then those who were in the boat came and worshiped him, saying, "Truly you are the Son of God." (NKJV, slightly altered)

'*Jesus made his disciples*—which means, Jesus compelled his disciples—to *get into the boat and go before him to the other side.*' He made them, he compelled them to go their own way without him, while he was somewhere else. They probably didn't understand what he wanted of them. It probably wasn't what they wanted. But that was of no consequence for them: they allowed what they were told to be right for them and they did it; they obeyed. And this already tells us something decisive about ourselves, who are Jesus' disciples, his church. This tells us that the church of Jesus Christ is the place where there is a bond which regulates human activity, a bond which cannot be debated over, which we have not chosen for ourselves, and from which we cannot release ourselves, but on the other hand a bond in which we also have the security and consolation which enable us to go on our own way as we should. Disciples of Jesus are people who are answerable to Jesus, and precisely for that reason answerable to no one else, people who are entirely bound, and precisely for that reason and in that bond, free people.

'*And when he had sent the multitudes away, he went up on the mountain alone to pray. Now when evening came, he was alone there.*' We may well ask whether this sovereignty, this command, this obedience, this allegiance we have just heard about might not also exist somewhere else in the world. Is the church really the only place where something like this happens? Or do we not find something quite similar elsewhere too? To be sure, we find something similar elsewhere, but only something similar. And what happens here when this bond and this obedience occur is something quite distinctively different from whatever else there may be in the world that resembles it. Do you know why? It is not because of the people in the church, or their state of mind, or the way they act, but because of the one who is sovereign in the church and sovereign over these people. We will allow that small but infinitely significant word, "alone," which we have just heard twice, to tell us who is sovereign over these people: "he went up on the mountain *alone* to pray. Now when the evening came, he was *alone* there." In the gospels we often read about Jesus Christ being alone like this. And wherever we read about it, it is an indication that Jesus is the one who is always utterly alone; and indeed, he is alone, alone in the way that God alone is. There were and are and will be great and significant people besides him as well. But what is a significant person? It is, in fact, a person whose personality is capable of signifying quite different and higher things beyond itself, of pointing to the mysteries and truths beyond human life which a person glimpses at longingly and hopefully. Happy are we that such significant people exist who can signify in this way. But Jesus does not signify. He is. And what can be seen in him are not great things of some kind or another, even the greatest things, but the Lord God himself. And the Lord God is not only seen in him; rather, he himself, this man, is the Lord our God. And God is not merely present here beyond the bounds of human life but truly in human life, in the life of a human person like us, directly in the form in which we live and die, present as a human being in our human history. And lo and behold, it is because he is this Son of God and son of man that he is completely and utterly alone, and in that sense an incomparable man. And he is also alone in what he does. For as we heard: he went off on his own like this in order to *pray*. This individual is what he is—he is God and man—in order that here among us and for our sake the following would take place on earth: God would be sought and found and glorified here by humankind. If that does not happen, then both the world and humankind are lost. And this praying, this seeking and finding, this glorifying of God is what none of us can do. In order that it should happen, God sent his Son to become human. Jesus is the one who travels this road, who forges the way from humankind to God. We could not do this. He has done it. He prayed, "Father, into your hands I commend my spirit!" And what happened there happened once and for all, and for the sake of all of us. It accomplished in eternity what for our sake had to happen. It saved us from sin and death. And the only one who did this is Jesus, and so he alone is our Lord: an incomparable sovereign. We talk of a sovereignty, a command, an obedience, a willingness and allegiance unlike any other, because in him we meet a *sovereign* unlike any other. When Jesus rules *God* rules, and God rules when *Jesus* rules. That is why this sovereignty is quite unlike any other sovereignty, and why there is no other obedience on earth like this one.

'But the boat was now in the middle of the sea, tossed by the waves, for the wind was contrary.' Indeed, friends, because this Jesus, and he alone, is God's Son, those who belong to him, his disciples, the members of his church—who are not what he is, but are only human—must go their own way on this earth. In the first place they are completely and utterly separated from him and have to fend for themselves. The church of Jesus

Christ in the world—oh, what is it, this church? Must we not continually acknowledge that it is no different than any of those many other more or less good and hopeful human ventures? But especially full of sin and especially threatened because people are attempting something especially bold here: to proclaim the truth about the true God, to serve and worship this God! How could humankind in all its dubiousness and all its defencelessness emerge any more clearly than it does here? And how could this venture not continually be met by difficulties from the inside and from without? And how could this venture not secretly be afflicted, and in a particularly intense and severe way at certain moments in time such as the one in which we are now living? What remains of the church then? Where should it turn? What is to become of Jesus' disciples when they find themselves in exactly the same boat as the rest of humanity? They are no better off or stronger than the rest, no less lost and helpless than the world as a whole; indeed, more lost and helpless, perhaps, than all the rest. "The wind was contrary." What do they have of Jesus to hold on to now? Surely only a memory? The memory of his word and the expectation of his help. But how weak our memory often is, and how weak this expectation! What else can we do, then, but cling to what has been given us, cling to the word, and, in spite of our weak attempts at remembering and hoping, to be obedient as far as our ability and understanding allow!

'*Now in the fourth watch of the night Jesus came to them, walking on the sea.*' Dear friends! It is because he alone, the true God and true man, is our helper and saviour, that what we hear about here happens and must happen: he does not leave his

49

people to themselves, he has not forgotten them. He has sent them on their way with a promise: Lo, I am with you always, even unto the end of the world! But we should certainly recall that it is grace, it is free grace, it is always an almighty act of the free grace of God, when this promise is fulfilled. He is not bound to us, but he comes to us. He comes to us where and when he wishes. And then that is always an *event* of his goodness. And this goodness of his which we hear about is an event that will continually encounter us as something *new*, an event which, God knows, we have never earned and which we may for our part neither expect nor demand, nor is it an event we can count upon, and it does not simply follow as a matter of course in our life or as a consequence of human history. No, when it comes, it stands before us as a divine miracle.

'*He came to them, walking on the sea.*' Jesus came to them. Is the event which is described here supposed to be entirely unfamiliar to us? Are we to be permitted to say, especially in this day and age: that happened there and then, but we have no knowledge of it!? Is it not the case that this Jesus has really and truly come to us too in these years, just as he did then to the disciples in the storm? Is it not true that in these years we have had the unexpected surprise of learning and perceiving something we didn't previously know about the majesty and matchlessness of divine revelation, about the terrible seriousness of sin, but also of how delightful the obedience is which we owe to the Lord, and something of what the church is and what confession might mean? If that is so, if perhaps we have glimpsed even only a tiny glimmer of all this in recent days, then lo and behold it has happened among us too: Jesus came to them, walking on the sea! A divine miracle. And in spite of everything that can weigh on our hearts, it would be ungrateful of us not to confess above all else—gratefully to confess—that he is indeed here with us, along with his Spirit and gifts!

'And when the disciples saw him walking on the sea, they were troubled, saying, "It is a ghost!" And they cried out for fear.' What has happened then? Jesus came to them. And they, his people, don't recognise him. They don't realise that it is he who is coming towards them, but think they are seeing a ghost—which in this context means a figment of their imagination—and they are afraid and cry out. To be sure, if it were really a figment of their imagination, a ghost, which they had encountered here, they would certainly have had cause to be afraid. A Jesus who is not really Jesus but a figment of the pious imagination, the product of our revolutionary or reactionary dreams, the mirage of our hopelessness or our enthusiasm—a Jesus like this certainly may and must be feared, for in fact this imaginary Jesus could only magnify the distress we experience in our lives and in the church. If this is an imaginary Jesus, or a ghost, there is certainly reason to be afraid, for then the turmoil human beings are in can, without fail, only increase. And the more passionately this Jesus is believed and proclaimed, the deeper will be the distress, the darker the night in which the church finds itself. Better no Jesus at all than a ghost like that, a figment of the imagination.

'But immediately Jesus spoke to them, saying, "Be of good cheer! It is I; do not be afraid."' Isn't it true that we want to ask how we can be sure that it is really Jesus who is coming, and not a phantom we have dreamed up or imagined? If we wish to obtain certainty over this, if we wish to know whether it is really Jesus

Christ, the Son of God himself, that we are dealing with in our faith, our proclamation, in the word that is spoken, heard and believed in the church, then we are certainly not to look inside our own hearts. It cannot be a question of examining our consciences or measuring the depth or the fire or the spirit of our convictions, but of one thing alone, which is not located within ourselves but is the decision taken by him, by Jesus Christ himself. And that occurs when what we have just heard about takes place: "Immediately Jesus spoke to them!" Immediately! We need not be afraid. When the time comes he will begin to speak and will tell us what we must hear. He will address us. Jesus is not merely a blind force which just operates and is simply to be felt. Let us not trust our feelings one bit, but wait to hear the word he has for us. What is Jesus telling us? 'Be of good cheer!' Which means, You may dare to count and build on the fact I am he who is present with you; you may dare to defy your fear and to believe, to grasp hold of me; you may do that! If we have heard this "You may!" we have heard *his* voice. And he says, "It is I, do not be afraid!" Do not be afraid of what can assail you as human beings, both outside and from within, within yourselves! And do not be afraid of the evil that can and perhaps must appear when you surrender to your own imagination and call upon images of God, images of Jesus, which you yourselves have made! Do not be afraid, it is I! And because it is I who am speaking with you, helplessness and fear vanish, the figments of your imagination vanish, this false Jesus vanishes into the wind in a puff of smoke: I, the real Jesus, stand before you; and because it is I you needn't be afraid! This is how Jesus addresses us. And if you say to me, "Indeed, but isn't there always still room for error; couldn't the voice of our own hearts always try to pass itself off as the voice of Jesus Christ?" then my reply is, "We may and must continually seek the word, the conclusive word of Jesus Christ himself, in the word to which the prophets and apostles are witnesses, the word of those who for every age have born testimony to him, to his revelation, to his work, to the love of God which has appeared in him." And whoever hears this testimony to him knows that he himself is there, that the light is there, the truth is there, the victory is there; not a human victory but God's victory in his church, even in such times of tribulation and division as we are now living through. We can be sure that the victory is always on the side of Holy Scripture, and so it is today. The members of his body and of his church are to be found where his word, just as it was received by his witnesses, is once again received and heard by us too. "He who hears you hears me." In that case, even today: "It is I."

'And Peter answered him and said, "Lord, if it is you, command me to come to you on the water.'" Something new and unexpected now takes place. Lo and behold, one of Jesus' disciples now steps forward out of the crowd, one who is apparently daring to do, and therefore to be, something special. Have you heard this? Here is someone who expects a specific word from Jesus directed specifically to him. What is going on inside this man Peter? Clearly, what is going on is that he says to himself, "Jesus has me in mind when he utters the words, 'Be of good cheer! It is I; do not be afraid!'" This has not simply been addressed to people in general; nor is it simply heard by everyone. It is *I* who have heard it, and no matter what others might make of it, *I* have heard it and *I* am to follow this call and be, at this point

in time, the one to whom this word is directed and addressed. And so Peter makes this strange request of Jesus, that he should command him to come to him on the water. What does that signify? Is it pride that makes him want to attempt this peculiar thing? There is so much religious pride that will easily inflate a person when he imagines he has been called: I am the one, I must do it! He thinks he's been given permission to make an exhibition of his righteousness, when in fact he hasn't. Is that it? Or is Peter acting here out of the seriousness of a living faith? One might well ask. In his interpretation of these words, Calvin decided that it was indeed more an act of pride on the part of Peter, who overrated his faith by attempting to pull off this stunt which would advance his own interests by outshining everyone else. It must be admitted that the attitude we have just seen him adopt certainly casts him in a strangely sinister light. And yet we should take note that Peter does not simply embark on something without further ado, but addresses Jesus with the words, "Command me to come to you on the water!" That is, he waits on an order from Jesus, and only on the basis of this order will he proceed. At any rate, he makes his interests a matter for Jesus' will *as well*, even if we will agree that something like pride must also have been involved, as Calvin suggests. For the whole history of the church has always taken a course such that one could certainly ask whether such-and-such a person is acting out of arrogance and vanity and pride, or out of a profound and serious faith. The great decisions in the church have always been taken under this cloud, both in the early church and during the time of the Reformation, and it cannot be any different today either. And yet in spite of every obstacle, decisions have often been reached under this cloud, one way or another, which God has blessed. And one way or another, it was often not *only* hubris, vanity and arrogance—and indeed even the most noble and superior personality is not rid of these—which led someone to dare to do what Peter was attempting here, but the hidden and yet clear will of God on these occasions, so that those concerned had to do what they did. Peter, who emerges here in this murky light, asked Jesus for this order. And it is of this Peter that Christ said, "On this rock I will build my church!" What is required—what Jesus Christ continually requires—are rocks like this who are certainly not perfectly untainted people, who are perhaps seriously objectionable in many ways and will have much to answer for, but are nevertheless ready to do something quite specific, to render obedience to a specific word by undertaking a specific service. In the church of Jesus Christ there is not only waiting, there must also be those individuals who are continually hastening, watching, rising where they are called to, with all the perils that entails. The church could not do without them, and the church cannot do without them today either. And now in this hour, the text puts this question to each and every one of us: And you, are you not also called to obey in a *specific* way? To be sure, we must examine ourselves to see whether we are ready to obey the orders of *Jesus Christ*, or whether the appeal we are now hearing might not come from some chimera within our hearts. But equally, let us examine ourselves to see whether it is not the result of our cowardice and *unbelief* if we do *not* assume this specific task, this specific act of obedience to which we are summoned!

'So he said, "Come." And when Peter had come down out of the boat, he walked on the water to go to Jesus.' It has now happened, and however things might have been for Peter beforehand, the order of Jesus Christ has now gone out to him. And he dares to carry it out and succeeds: he walks on the water. And now this Peter is indeed a distinguished man. He is distinguished because he has been allowed to participate in the glory of Jesus Christ, distinguished because of the greater *demands* that have been made on him (greater than those made on his brothers!), indeed distinguished too by the greater *temptation* he now faces. But he is also distinguished by the greater *help* which comes his way. There is distinction like this in the church: people who are distinguished by what is demanded of them, distinguished by the dangers to which they expose themselves, but also distinguished by the help that comes their way. And distinction like this, a specific event like this, has always been the mystery of the great periods of the Christian church. Is it the case that distinction like this is to be granted to us too in these days and years, to us, to our evangelical church, in that from the midst of everything that bears the name of church, a crowd has dared to step out in obedience and become the confessing church? Our thoughts always are and were clouded by that great uncertainty: Is it him, or is it the illusion of our hearts? But the word of Jesus was and is in our ears, and we did not think, nor do we, that we could flinch from being ready at his side. Yes, that is what we believe—how else should we attempt what we are daring to do?—and we may also consider that in times like this everything seems to become greater than it ever was before: the demands, the dangers, the temptation, but also the help. Happy are we if this is the case!

But what an immeasurable responsibility we have if it is! How we would have to cherish God's blessing, how loyal we would have to remain then, how humble and courageous we would have to be in clinging on to what God has given us, and perhaps will give us yet!

'But when he saw that the wind was boisterous, he was afraid; and beginning to sink he cried out, saying, "Lord, help me!"' Yes, that is what can happen. That is what has always happened. That is how it ends up. In the times of great grace, this is what human beings are like when they are confronted by the great displays of God's grace. What has become of Peter now? He is no different to the person who set such store by following Jesus' orders in daring to do something as bold as this. He is the same man. He would still like to come to Jesus. It is just that one thing has now happened: he doesn't just pay heed to this coming, but catches sight of something else too, namely the storm. And he is afraid. He doesn't just believe—he also says, "Yes, I believe, yes of course I do!" But in doing so, he asks, "Is this really working? Can I really do it? Can I manage this, given the storm as well?" These are serious questions for one who has dared to obey. Oh, if only Peter would reflect that, however serious they may be, all these serious questions are already answered by the glory of Jesus Christ, who called out to him and who enables him to discover who he is! If only he would just keep on paying heed to Jesus alone, rather than looking out for the storm! But no sooner does he do that than this little "and" appears: Jesus *and* the storm, Jesus *and* practical considerations, Jesus *and* the question of how one is to do this and to see it through; Jesus *and* my helplessness or my hopes and desires and my many human problems. As soon

as this little "and" comes on the scene, all is lost. What takes hold in that moment is what took hold then: fear. Fear of the real world and fear of the boldness of one's own attempt. Dear friends, do you realise this? Has anyone ever told you, and have you allowed yourself to be told, that it is impossible to believe *and* to worry? When a person believes, he can do nothing *but* believe and, in believing, cast all his cares upon the Lord. If he thinks things are different, he is precisely *not* believing, and then he is surely lost, which means that the situation turns out as we see it does here. For then things really don't work out in *practice* either, and he fails in reality too. He loses his footing altogether and can no longer help himself, and then those long debates and those little crises come along again so that he has reverted to what he was when he set out. The power of the Lord both inside and out has left him again and he is reduced to the small person he was when he embarked on this course, a little too troubled and a little too impractical. And then—well, then the game is up. And apparently it turns out that it was not faith at all that drove him, but only pride. And then? Then things happen just as we are told they do. "He began to sink!" And he could do nothing but cry out, "Lord help me!" What is described for us here is the history of every great event in the church. Whenever disaster strikes the church, this consists quite simply in people not having believed enough. Oh, but their faith was always so strong, so bold and passionate! And yet, what was disastrous was that while they believed, they always kept on glancing over to one side, where it was no longer a matter of Jesus but of the storm, of practical and strategic matters, of oneself and one's desires and crises, of human affairs and the way of the world. If they had *only* believed, it would not even have been necessary to be so bold and strong of faith! A grain of corn would have had the strength to move mountains. If we think we can believe *and* at the same time feel we must continue to steal glances like this, then to be sure, the church's cause is lost once again, and it must suffer affliction and shame.

'And immediately Jesus stretched out his hand and caught him, and said to him, "O you of little faith, why did you doubt?"' This is good for us to hear. For now we are told that even if disasters like this should occur—and these disasters *do* occur again and again, for these are the sort of Christians we *are*, this *is* what the church is like, and what Jesus' disciples are like; this is what they *do*, and they *do* disgrace themselves in this manner—be that as it may, the principle and most important thing is that all is not yet lost. Oh, all would certainly have been lost many times over if it had depended on us human beings behaving differently than Peter does here. Even if Peter sinks, that does not mean that Jesus Christ does. And as long as Jesus does not sink, Peter cannot go under entirely either, if he remembers this one thing: that he is now to rely directly and uniquely on *Jesus*. Indeed, even when Christians fail, even those who are distinguished associates of God, they still continue to be called on that account, and both their service and their task remain. God's greatest servants have disgraced God and brought affliction upon the church. But God has *not* abandoned those who belong to him on account of that. Even if we are unfaithful, he is faithful, and the one thing we need to do is to consider this and, when we are at our wits' end, wholeheartedly to cry out to him saying, "Help me, Lord!" And then we must be told, "O you of little faith, why did you

doubt?" But to tell us this is already to help us as well, for Peter was called, after all, and the church is after all the church. And it is precisely because of this that Peter is and remains called, and that the church remains God's church, even in its shameful affliction. And because this cry issues from the deepest distress, a cry which is really only an appeal for God's merciful grace, something can now be made of it. No longer is it a bold venture and mission. It is now a matter of taking a step back from making haste, and of waiting in order to receive the strength to perform new deeds. For it is undoubtedly true that Jesus Christ allows his people to become weak so that they can then become truly strong. "He stretched out his hand and caught him." This reaching for Peter who was already lost, humanly speaking, is the most glorious tonic, the greatest help, and furnishes the most powerful authority imaginable. As such it always benefits the *weak*. And then this weak individual is stronger than the strongest man in the world. This is how the church is restored. It is always God who restores it, without and even contrary to our efforts, if only we human beings will know and believe that it is he who helps us.

'And when they got into the boat, the wind ceased. Then those who were in the boat came and worshiped him, saying, "Truly you are the Son of God."' We have heard, dear friends, how everything we have learned was said *by us* and therefore *to us*. Christ going off to be alone, Jesus coming to his own people, the word he utters to reveal who he is, his call to Peter, and Peter's triumph and defeat and the further help he receives—everything, the whole lot, is spoken by us and for our sake. But everything depends on us now joining together with those who are on the

boat and saying with them, "Truly you are the Son of God!" On no account will we ever accomplish as Christians, as our Lord's church, what we have to do, however rightly we go about it. Neither the church that slumbers nor the church that stays awake, neither the living church nor the church that has fallen away from Scripture and confession, nor the confessing church either, will manage it. Rather, what is fitting for us to do, fitting to the extent that it is the one thing we had to do, and which in Jesus Christ has already been done, is to belong to God. The one thing *we* can do is this: looking away from ourselves, to cry and sigh and rejoice in gratitude and cheerful humility, "Truly you are the Son of God, you alone!" If only we would learn to place all our confidence in this one thing—Truly you are the Son of God, you our Saviour, you!—continually allowing all our faith, all our hope and all our love to be nothing but this one thing: You! It is the church that has received the promise which cries out like this, and the gates of hell shall not prevail against it.

Afterword

When Pastor Kurt Johanson discovered that Karl Barth's famous sermon on the Titanic had never been published in German or English, he called the Center for Barth Studies to find out how he could get hold of a copy. The origins of this slim volume go back to that phone call.

The Center for Barth Studies was founded at Princeton Theological Seminary in 1997 not only to promote research on the world-famous Swiss-German theologian, but also to connect Barth scholars across the world. In the ten years since its founding, the Center has collaborated on research projects of various kinds with scholars in Germany, The Netherlands, Switzerland, and South Africa, among other places. These collaborations have enabled us to connect scholars from various regions of the world. So it happened that a pastor in Dallas, Texas got permission from a board of trustees in Basel, Switzerland to enlist a doctoral candidate in London, England to translate not only the "Titanic" sermon but also Barth's 1934 sermon on Matthew 14:22–33. We at the Center are happy that we could play a small role in bringing these two contrasting specimens of Barth's homiletic to an English-speaking audience.

Our hope is that more of Barth's sermons will be published in English in the coming years. His most accessible and widely read collections are *Deliverance to the Captives!* and *Call for God*, which he preached in the Basel prison in the late 1950s and early 1960s. *Come, Holy Spirit* and *God's Search for Man*, volumes of sermons which he published in collaboration with his good friend and fellow pastor, Eduard Thurneysen, are also available in English. However, a wealth of new sermons has been published in recent years in the *Karl Barth Gesamtausgabe* [Karl Barth Collected Edition]. Scholars who read German now have access to almost all of the sermons Barth preached over the course of his career: nearly four hundred sermons from his pastoral ministry in Safenwil and approximately one hundred and thirty preached while he was teaching at his various academic posts in Germany and Switzerland. Soon all of his nearly seven hundred sermons will be published. Some intrepid scholars have already begun working on this wealth of new material. Our hope is that more of these sermons will soon be translated and thus made more accessible to pastors and students in the English-speaking world. The study of his sermons will undoubtedly change our understanding of Barth's theological path in subtle and perhaps significant ways.

In the meantime, we at the Center for Barth Studies are thankful that Pastor Johanson has whetted our appetite for what is to come by publishing these fascinating sermons.

Clifford B. Anderson
Curator of Special Collections
Princeton Theological Seminary

Contributors

CLIFFORD B. ANDERSON is Curator of the Special Collections at Princeton Theological Seminary.

CHRISTOPHER ASPREY is a doctoral candidate at the University of Aberdeen, Scotland.

GEOFFREY W. BROMILEY is the English translator of Karl Barth's *Church Dogmatics* and author of *An Introduction to the Theology of Karl Barth*.

EBERHARD BUSCH is Professor Emeritus of Systematic Theology on the Faculty of Theology at the University of Goettingen and author of numerous books and articles on Karl Barth.

KURT I. JOHANSON is Pastor at Pleasant Grove Church in Dallas, Texas and adjunct lecturer in Homiletics at Dallas Christian College, Dallas, Texas.

DONALD K. MCKIM is Academic and Reference Editor at Westminster John Knox Press and editor of *How Karl Barth Changed My Mind*.

BRUCE E. SHIELDS is Blowers Professor of Christian Ministries at Emmanuel School of Religion in Johnson City, Tennessee.

JAMES D. STRAUSS is Professor Emeritus of Theology and Philosophy at Lincoln Christian Seminary, Lincoln, Illinois.

WILLIAM H. WILLIMON is Bishop of the North Alabama Conference of the United Methodist Church and Visiting Professor at Duke Divinity School. He is the author of *Conversations with Barth on Preaching* (Abingdon, 2006).

DIETER ZELLWEGER, grandson of Karl Barth, is President of the Karl Barth Legacy Commission.

Printed in the United States
151190LV00002B/64/A